Seven *and* Deadly

Vice and Virtue Behind the Veil

MARIAM ANWAR MOLANI

RIVER GROVE
BOOKS

Published by River Grove Books
Austin, TX
www.rivergrovebooks.com

Distributed by River Grove Books

Design and composition by Greenleaf Book Group
Cover design by Greenleaf Book Group
Cover images ©Adobe Stock/Mari Dein; ©Adobe Stock/Oleksandra

Publisher's Cataloging-in-Publication data is available.

Print ISBN: 978-1-966629-93-1

eBook ISBN: 978-1-966629-94-8

First Edition

Praise for
Seven and Deadly

Eviscerating, sharp, and darkly witty, this book is a blade. With surgical precision, Molani lays her readers bare.

—**JOY SULLIVAN**, author of
Instructions for Traveling West

Poems in *Seven and Deadly* are intimate whispers, defiant slogans and lyrical revelations. Molani's voice is utterly original; it sings on the page. A truly wondrous debut.

—**MOHAMMED HANIF**,
author of *Rebel English Academy*

Both visceral and sophisticated, *Seven and Deadly* is a collection that will quickly catch hold of you and pull you in with its short but complex snippets of raw emotion. Molani's voice is a mix of Warsan Shire and Miroslav Holub; she is fierce and uninhibited, buttressed by scientific precision and wonder. These verses are about womanhood, life in color, and the collision of modern and ancient longings. Like the world's favorite vices, these poems go down easy and will leave your thumb itching to flip the pages back for another taste.

—**VERA HERBERT**, Film and TV writer,
Don't Make Me Go, This Is Us

*For the gloriously flawed
and functionally unrepentant*

Contents

WRATH

Bitterness is like cancer. It eats upon the host.
But anger is like fire. It burns it all clean.

—Maya Angelou

Can you be born
needing revenge?
Can you inherit blood
steeped in the fury
of foremothers?

—*succession*

At this point
I do not believe in
men and women
masculine or feminine
XX or XY
I believe only in
alphas and betas
the surf and the shore
wolves and sheep

—*revelations*

I wonder if I am a little broken
or missing a few lines of code
What other reason can I have
for this festering rage?
Could this be the same breeze
under which others sail so placidly
that stokes the dry tinder
beneath my soles into wildfire
scorching
demented
all-consuming?

—going up in flames

I was told that
women should be soft and supple
like the boughs of a willow,
but I found that soft bellies
are easily pierced
and delicate skin flayed, so
I built myself
piece by piece
of bricks and mortar
to withstand the lash
of tongue and talon
I will not be taken prisoner
in my own home

—*fortress of flesh and bone*

Does it make me unhinged
that I would rather feel the blade of reality at
    my throat
than bathe in the heady perfume of delusion?
Does it make me irredeemable
that my body stands unbent before altars built
for false gods created by false men?
Does it make me insurgent
if I see the world through clear eyes
and not the cunning shroud of tradition
made to control and subdue?
Does it make me derelict
if I demand volition unencumbered by
the weight of decorum and duty?
Does it make me ungrateful
if I choose to dissect the knowledge
fed to my malnourished body
rather than consume it to relieve
the ache of incessant hunger?

—inquisition

Growing up
I was told one should not hate
What word should I use then
to describe what I feel
for a world that feasts on innocence
and delights in pain?
I've tried *despise, loathe, abhor*
but they leave me wanting
Maybe it's the bite of the *t*
that encapsulates
the force of the defilement
the bitterness of its aftertaste
the hot brand of violence
and wounds that fester . . .
This is hate's shining moment
the reason for which it was created
All in favor?
It is *ayes* around the table
and the word *hate*
keeps its seat

—parliamentary procedure

I come from a martial race
of women who do not
succumb to admiration nor
submit to fear
but rather
whet daggers in the dark
keep secrets and
tell lies with unwavering gazes
to guard smoke
curling from kindling of
gods-given dreams

—sentinel

It is not submission
if we are held
prostrate with swords
to our backs
blood in our mouths
Our spines curve to shield
this unrepentant organ that beats in our chest
Though bodies grow weary,
resolve remains keen
we will
hold
hold
hold
We are used to the wait

—defensive strategy

You speak of wrath and women scorned
but name me something more
Vitriolic
Volatile
Violent
Vengeful
than a man who
fears a woman

—I'll wait

and what of us
who were made of damp earth
and honeycomb?
The ones who do not speak
the language of cruelty and soot,
but converse in the dialects
of sea foam, clematis,
and the steady hum
of unfettered wings?
Would we succumb,
levied under the reign of Chaos
mouths gagged
eyes veiled in ash
forced to march
alongside legions
of malice and despair?

—*prisoners of war*

Some people are bricks in the desert
silently absorbing the heat of the world
hunched and haunted
by red-hot weight

Then, when all is still
and others drift into dreamless slumber
Despair erupts like a kettle of screams
and billows out in pulses of panic

Until in the deep of night
Sleep suffocates her
and she surrenders,
slipping for a moment
into the respite
of the cool black

—just before the dawn

To have taken an oath
to do no harm
in a world that insists
on perpetuating it,
is the heartbreak
I may never recover from

—on toxic relationships

You say women are
hopeless with directions
I'm inclined to agree
We have done a piss-poor job
navigating this world
with a blindfold over our eyes,
mislabeled maps in our hands,
every voyage fraught with torrent and gale
Still in the maelstrom,
a thought strikes me—
It's almost as if
you never wanted us to get there

—saboteur

I despise the color pink,
but it reassures him
and he reassures me
I have never looked so lovely

—*notes on androcracy*

———◦◦◇◦◦———

Ha! You want me
to trust those who,
during the birth of a nation
withheld life, liberty,
and the pursuit of happiness
from those who had
birthed the nation?

—*once bitten*

Don't talk to me of tradition—
He is the reason why
my grandmother learned
how to reproduce
before she learned
how to read

—*persona non grata*

and if even one woman
remains bound and gagged
on this earth,
so are we all

—*domino theory*

The nice thing about
becoming feral
is that you forget
to fear

—metamorphosis,
sunny-side up

PRIDE

*I do not care so much what I am to others
as I care what I am to myself.*

—Michel de Montaigne, *Essays ("Of Glory")*

How many times must you take the higher
    road before you perish from the climb?

—descent

———◦◦◇◦◦———

My feminism is
diaphanous—
you recoil quickly
when you see
your own likeness
rear its head
and bare its teeth

—fractures in façade

My husband told me yesterday
that he was surprised I had written a poem
all in one sitting
For all my words, I cannot find
the right ones to explain
that poems aren't built
they are birthed—
erupting in a gush of zinc and salt
through gritted teeth and heart chambers
distended with nostalgia
How do I tell him that these verses
are not curated or crafted
but sprung forth
like Athena from the head of Zeus?
One day, floating in a swell of dreams
the next, bubbling over like hot milk
spilling from the ether
onto paper
into being

—*genesis*

I don't want to be
the soft sanctum
he buries his head in
when he faces defeat
I want to be
the knife
he reaches for
when he wants
to draw blood

—up in (his) arms

Try as we might to thwart her,
Biology has a slender hand
around our neck
and a macabre sense of humor—
We need little goading
to act like beasts

—primitive

I feel so ordinary
and I cannot understand why I feel
such a *compulsion*
to be extraordinary
what would I need to achieve
to become impressive to myself?
For the time being I am banal, superfluous,
and drowning in my own mediocrity

—invisible woman

Unveiled

My husband is reading my poems. I sit next to him, tense, picking at a flake of skin along my cuticle as I ready myself to dissect his facial expressions. I've peeled myself open and invited him to take a bite—I brace for the pain of rejection.

Goose pimples erupt along my skin. He is the first to read these hesitant fractals of my soul. I feel naked. Why does sharing poetry feel more intimate than sex?

I peer at him through the corner of my eye, wondering how a normal person contends with signs of catalyzing entropy. Have I divulged too much or did he always suspect? Can white men who have captained their vessels in the deep, calm waters of privilege navigate the seething spume of a tropical storm? Could the Pacific ever comprehend the Dead Sea? Will he pause and look over at me with newfound regard or will this leave a stain—like blood on white sheets or betel nut on hot pavement?

I have learned that
for most people
out of sight is out of mind—
the antithesis to my own
A cavernous maw dripping
stalactites of memory
It is a bristling feeling,
this fungibility
No missed calls
no texts
just wallets full of negative film

—unrequited

Let me go,
after all,
how long should I carry
the weight of your absence?
How long should I wade in
cold waters
with bleary eyes
and pockets full of stone?

—mourning sickness

I am not currently offering
serial dilutions
Come back when you
can withstand the concentrate

—chemistry 101

He quietly slides over
a plate full of white flags
I'm sorry, they whisper
through puffs of steam
bourbon vanilla and the good cacao
bitter as the words
we just flung at each other
When water abandons my eyes for my mouth
I consider unshouldering the storm
My advisors, sparring partners
deliberate at length
What say you?
Just as Pride tosses up
her jaunty little chin
I feel a gentle tug on my hand
and Forgiveness implores,
Do not hold me hostage

—*reconciliation*

I want to read more,
so I can write more,
but the more I read
the less certain I am
that I can write

Do I need more
the reassurance of others?
Or my own praise?
For at the moment
I am desperately short on both

—Dunning-Kruger effect

Did my god forsake me
because I forsook her?

—petty

Where is the line
between confidence and delusion?
Within the pitch-dark
of dream and desire
I cannot find it
And, again, I must wonder—
is this by design?

—no man's land

<hr>

Trust me when I say
I set the bar this high
not just for you

—tyrant

It is frigid out here in your shadow
Apathy slicing like April wind

I came to your door
threadbare and starved
Faced your blunted gargoyle gaze
My knees are clacking, lips gone blue
How can you deny me
the warmth of your praise?

—*frostbite*

Triangles

Today, I learned that the most stable shape is a triangle. No soft edges, dips, or curves, just cold, hard lines and a triumvirate of points. They say triangles, both natural and manufactured, are resistant to deformation and manipulation under pressure. It is a triangle's rigidity that gives it strength, alongside the efficiency with which it redistributes stress when subjected to force. Sextets of triangles make tessellations; airtight strongholds with no waste, no nonsense. Triangles do the work. They can take some shit. Triangles *endure.* Triangles embody resilience, yet somehow also capture grace. Shark fins, bird beaks, cicada armor; spiral scales climb balsam cones. Deltas sing where river meets the sea. A sunflower boasts her seed lattice, a pineapple bats her eyes. Forest, plains, and marsh conspire and crown the mountain as queen. Her throne is granite, her will resolute, but I find myself wondering, is it lonely at the peak?

I am just out here
Subsisting
Existing
Resisting
Persisting

I don't quite
fit in
and for the first time in my life
I don't want to

—a modern guide to survival

SLOTH

———◇◇◇◇———

Nature does not hurry,
yet everything is accomplished.

—Lao Tzu, *Tao Te Ching*

I want to stop rolling
and quietly gather moss

—*stoned*

More and more
I enjoy the quiet
of my own company
I am the only
person around
whom all of these unapologetic facets
can *shine*

—*solitaire*

I've done nothing but laze today
under the influence of this Meyer-lemon sun
Ah, it's been divine
every moment of my crime
resting on sugared laurels
when there is so much
to be done

—*lemonade*

Dip me into a permafrost
like the Alaskan wood frog
Let the anesthesia creep
The berries are bitter
The lake has gone still
When I look to sojourners
who pass through my woods
all I see are hollowed cheeks

Wake me when the lupine thaws
Wake me in gentler times
For now, let me sleep
while cold has settled like dust
and hope has faded
like the light

—*forget-me-not*

I'd rather remain silent,
comfortable in my repose,
for why *should* I speak?
Inquire, and you are intrusive
Refute, and you are contentious
Deduce, and you are offensive
Propose, and you are unsolicited
Deny, and you are blasphemous
Flaunt, and you're a whore
Abstain, and you're a bore
What's the use of conversation anymore?

—*table for one*

Fog settles like summer cotton
over little hills that aspire to mountainhood
The morning tastes like brine
Today, I am aimless
a gull floating over the sea
a wan, uninspired puff of mist
There are times I fissure into
a kaleidoscope of colors
but for now, I remain unmoored on the current
blissfully, sinfully
adrift

—*resting potential*

I grow tired of peeling off
my skin after coming home
divoted from neutrality and smiles
benevolence and lipstick
and scavenging for a feminine gentleness
that grows scantier by the day
Here, in my refuge
I can shed my cloak and
expose my barbed flesh
with no collateral damage
at peace
alone
in the dark

—*peau d'orange*

I hear them,
but I don't understand them
Am I ahead of my time
or simply traveling in a different plane?

—*spaced out*

You may do it later, old friend
but later this Monet sunset
will have melted into dusk
and the children's tinkling laughter
will have faded into the long and somber
chords of late summer
Bubbles will have stilled, awaiting your toast
bread gone stale and coffee cold
Gears will have rusted beside
silvered crowns, patinaed bones
You can do it later, my dear
but I will pick my lilies
while I may

—*evanescent*

I apologize for
the neglect
I am not so much
taciturn as I am likely
to be devouring
the last rays of
this singular sunset
and crushing it
with my pestle
into poem

—*summer daze*

It's easier to be a cynic
than a hopeful
This much I know

What a fever dream!
To live unbothered
nestled at the breast of a nebular mist,
but gravity has proved a formidable teacher
Now my mouth is stuffed full of earth
ears ringing from the crash
My pilgrimage ad astra in vain
All that remains is a black hole in my chest
the same shape as the vestiges of my faith,
last seen floating
amidst the stardust

—*terminal velocity*

Beloved, you wanted forever,
but the earth will forget you
It is how it copes with your loss

—*legacy*

⸺⸱⸱⸱⸺

This morning I awoke
wanting to learn the names
of birds and ferns
So, I stifled a sob and
buried those dreams in a wet field
A requiem on my way to work
Now I am reduced to specter
in a gray stone cell
under fluorescent lights
where the wild cannot possibly find me
—*call of duty*

Is it a waste of time?
All this dreaming and longing and *aching*?
Or is it the point?

—questions over coffee

——◆——

I've never much cared for the levity of red—
it is the blues that have me
in a chokehold

—downcast

Is there any sound
more reassuring
than birdsong
in the morning
and a chorus of
cicadas at dusk?

—a piece of peace

⎯⎯◦∞◇∞◦⎯⎯

I set out to become a healer
and found myself needing
to be healed

—lost in wards and words

LUST

*To my soul: Are you ever going to
achieve goodness? . . . Ever be fulfilled, ever
stop desiring—lusting and longing for
people and things to enjoy?
Or for more time to enjoy them?*

—Marcus Aurelius, *Meditations*

Lies seem easy to swallow
Are they as easy to digest?
Their bodies ready, kneeling
mouths gaping, spit dripping
These guppies with empty bellies
and insatiable appetites
will eat anything to feel full

—alternate realities

Oh, the divine feminine
How rabid he is to
worship at her altar
He comes with oblations
of lotus, of silver, of cedar
honeyed hymns of devotion
rosewater promises and praise
so long as she remains silent
so long as she stands still
so long as she evades senescence
so long as she is
stone

—idolatry

You told me it was a ring
I didn't realize it went around my neck

—*collared*

<hr>

When we hunger for food
we are told it is sustenance,
cravings to make us whole
But if we hunger for companionship,
we are told it is depravity,
cravings that make us whores

—*requisites*

I once made a promise to
do no harm
I did not spare myself
but he offered me a cage so beautiful
I walked in with open arms

—*golden snare*

⸺◦◦◇◦◦⸺

Pretty thing that you were
I dove in headfirst
Permanent head injury now
Probably well-deserved

—*shallow end*

She was Aphrodite and knew it
oozing sex like a ripe split fig
Skin like dew, lips red velvet
Shirt, a weary warden
over two straining breasts

I concede he didn't stand a chance
had to turn and check
Did a double take so fast
(I) almost snapped his neck

—*involuntary manslaughter*

Sex is easy,
sex is everywhere,
but have you ever tasted
the sweet juice of
pure, unadulterated
sovereignty?

*—on things worth
     lusting after*

⸻ ◦◇◦ ⸻

Does your heart ache
reading these poems—
the way mine does when
words spill out of me like
     red wine on carpet?

—stained

and if tomorrow you lost your sight,
would your mirror mourn your loss?
All glory vanished
from eyes, skin, lips
What bodies would you covet
in the *tenebris*?

—*self-reflection*

Here I am
in all my gory

—*exposé*

I'm tired of this menu
the stale status quo
served with a side of
small minds and big mouths
too salty,
too bitter,
and generally uninspired

—RBF

I was told to use
God as an insurance policy,
but it's the Devil who helped me
love my body
when everyone else
tried to use it
He and I
are now friends

—devil's advocate

No creature longs for chains
but the doghouse is warm
The winter air, unforgiving
She howls at the moon in defeat

Abased or indebted?
Tell me again, I forget,
at which end of the leash is the beast?

—trauma-bond

I slip off my ring and
honey spills
down wagging tongues
silken and sweet
slick and searching

Courtesy is dead
Shared his brother's fate
Now only the mouthwatering
scent of possession
heals these hounds

—how to get good service
  at the bar

If you have time this week,
walk into your den
and crawl out an octopus
Show me eight ways you can
lend me a hand
Wade toward the sink
Reacquaint yourself with the dishes
before they become as dank as my mood
Fold the laundry
without turning red
Feed me something
without asking how or where
Turn off the game
without breaking any one of your hearts
And when the sun sets,
take me into your arms,
envelop me like the soft
flesh of an oyster
and sing me a lullaby
of the deep and the dark

—*aphrodisiac*

ENVY

---

*I am jealous of everything whose
beauty does not die.*

—**Oscar Wilde,** *De Profundis*

I wonder what it's like
to be lauded for unapologetic truth
Everything I say to myself
goes through rounds of editing
and, even then, the reception
is lukewarm

—*peanuts in the gallery*

I wish, like you
I, too, could wade into
the shallows
puffing
preening
but, alas, I am anchored
in the depths

—*seaworthy*

Envy is conniving
He arrived quietly, donned in green
The color of cypress, silk moth
moonflower vine
The color of guileless things

I faced the mirror
choked, revulsed
at the pile of putrid pulp

The remorseless wraith had consumed me like
a late-stage malignancy

—*preying mantis*

Oh, to be born with
big bones and white skin!
It's a heady combination
No wonder you seem
intoxicated

—omnipotence

⸺◦◦◇◦◦⸺

I wear him like a shield
all white skin and phallus
Few can name a better talisman
to ward off such
hate, contempt, and
evil
that skin such as mine
ignites

—protected?

All the other girls are in Italy,
no cellulite on their yacht
Bubbles on the bottom,
twenty-four in the middle
double Ds on top

Pledge, turn, prestige
Confusion
A sultry voice whispers, look again
it's an illusion

Well hand them an Oscar!
Give them the gold!
I bought every single story they sold

Now just looking for a pill to cure
   this delusion

—*highlight* ~~*real*~~ *reel*

This angst is unbearable
I should have loved to be a Libra

—*crabby*

⸺⸺◇◇◇◇◇⸺⸺

Above all,
I envy their complacence
Carafes of Cava,
cloudless skies
What an effervescent way of life
to be so weightless—
blind, deaf, and dumb
unbothered by the tumult of the world
Do you know how
tiresome it is
to always care?

—*chronic fatigue*

I rebuke it!
Rebuke it!
This feeling that has forever mired
the sluggish cisterns of my chest
The bones in my feet are broken
from walking in their shoes
and the path before me
winds beyond my sight
How I wish I could unyoke myself
join the others at ease,
buoyant
blithe
a glass of wine in my hand
and my head thrown back in laughter

—*five o'clock*

Like feathered sails of gold and blue
how I long to shine
the vibrance, the vanity,
ostentation worth the dime

but there is earth caked beneath my claws
and many nights I have not slept
bruised orbs set beneath my brow
wings slick with shadow and sweat

The truth is, glittering takes work
and I have spent all my coin on ink

Anyway, few would notice
the iridescent wings of a blackbird
in a land of peacocks and pink

—merle

In the meatiest part of summer
when berries flaunt their
sweet temperament
luscious curves
and heavy bottoms
do not avert your gaze
sodden with envy
Press your lips
to the fresh juice and
drink

—*green goddess*

Tempest

I am, by evolution or by the stars under which I was born, in a state of quiet chaos. Shakespeare might call me a tempest in a teapot, for inside me, there is always much ado about something.

I hide it well. I'm a decent conversationalist, and I know when to flash a smile that mostly reaches my eyes. But I am so often far away, and my words are seldom truthful; or, rather, they do not much reflect my truth. When someone asks me, "Hey, how are you today?" I respond light-heartedly, as obliged by social decorum and not to alarm the unsuspecting of the bedlam inside, and say, "I'm fine, and you?"

When what I'm really dying to say is, "I'm devastated to find out that out of the fifty-two propagations of the string-of-pearls succulent I had painstakingly pressed into perlite and soil five weeks ago, none have stayed to grow with me. I'm ill after seeing the brains of a pregnant woman smeared across a sidewalk somewhere in Palestine. I'm starving for summer but am manacled to the edges of a cool spring. I'm unwell because, instead of coffee, I swallowed my own bile this morning while reading an article about a mother who threw her two children out of a car moving at seventy-five miles an hour on a highway. The baby didn't make it. Neither did my breakfast, after reading that."

I want to declare that I'm angry that I bought a book of poetry, and I have not yet gotten to read it because I'm waiting to find a moment of peace to do it justice, but that doesn't seem to exist around here. I'm heartbroken because an old friend of mine died at thirty-four of a heart attack, and I wonder, how much sorrow and cortisol did he subsist on, to make his heart leave its post so soon? I'm unhappy because I realize that my parents are getting older and I can't imagine a world in which I exist and they don't. I'm hungry because instead of eating this morning, I spent all my time tying yellow ribbons in my baby's hair and dancing with her before I took her to school. I'm frustrated because I don't think I kissed my husband today, and I know I often forget to because instead of paying attention to him, I'm listening to the tempest roar.

Most days, I find myself in a fugue state made of the pitter-patter of raindrops and the silent scream of emails and the squelch of maggots as they feast on unripe corpses. I'm gasping for air as I bob in a little pocket of ether, wondering if California poppies might still grow on the charred slopes of the hill behind my house and about how yet another priest raped a child under the protection and blessings of his God and what day I might steal time to scrub my daughter's potty-training underwear and how perfectly scrumptious the colors are inside of a watermelon radish.

I want to explain that I'm achy, not in the joints of my bones but in the seams of the chambers inside my chest, for all the kind thoughts that raced through my head but never graced my tongue, like the compliments I never gave to the people I love most. I'm exasperated because I want to explain to others that I'm not a pessimist, but that my tolerance for cruelty, indifference, and selfishness has expired, and I can no longer bear to spare pardons for those insistent on spreading malice like butter on warm bread. I'm exhausted because I think people think I'm aloof, but, really, the teapot is brewing so force-fully that I fear that if I don't keep this porcelain composure I might just crack and spill boiling feeling everywhere and inconvenience everyone by filling the air with ash and the smell of burning flesh.

I'm bruised, for all the times I was perceived as taciturn and cryptic because I cannot not embody my truth—the overwhelming feelings of beauty and joy and awe that flow through my very being each day—until I put a pen to paper. I'm confused because I thought I was supposed to be a healer, but most nights I have a fever dream that perhaps I am a writer, instead. I want to shout that though my shoulders are built like Atlas, I did not consent to carry this burden on my back, and I wonder more often than you, why I am unable to set it down.

My husband sees me float away and, in a flicker, his eyes ask, *Where did you go? Come back.*

And I do, just in time to catch someone asking, "How are you?"

So, I lie and say, "I'm fine."

GREED

It is the privilege of the gods to want nothing,
and of godlike men to want little.

—Diogenes of Sinope

I've arrived
but, wait—
Am I in the right place?
This cesspool of
apathy and antagonism
could not possibly be
the same adulthood
I so dearly wished for as a child

—coming of age

———◦◦◇◦◦———

They buried it in us so deeply
this rapacious need for riches

Is it any surprise that it took root?

—of all evil

The world is ugly
always out for blood
and I, such tempting prey

Don't fault me my baubles
curated in troves
sapphire, opal
platinum and gold

Dazzling distractions,
a glittering defense
Oh! That is pretty!
Let me go and collect

Makeshift shields
of crumbles of starshine,
ease the melancholia
help pass the time

After all
when it lunges for my neck, the world
should at least be inconvenienced
by my pearls
—*magpie*

and if you had to dissolve
to assimilate?
deceive for affluence?
decompose for opulence?
would you do it?
would it grant you peace
or rob you of it?

—*on Pyrrhic victories*

Does it give my skin more worth,
the fact that he has claimed me?
I couldn't be a thoroughbred,
had to settle for prize-pony

—*blue-ribbon Barbie*

A little more and I'll be happy
A little more and I'll be fine
But when I slit the belly of my
   patron goose
I found no golden eggs inside

—*wild goose chase*

The seat was never yours
they always said as much
but if you're not at the table,
you're assuredly on it

So, sharpen your nails and bare your teeth
If you want it, take it
Aim and leap
the jugular does not pulse for the weak

Claw it out of their fingers
and do not let guilt linger
for the fair fight they preached
of was myth

Pull up a chair, sit down, preside
before they filet you
muscle and hide
whistling as they hollow out
your insides

—*Y-incision*

Let me show you
all of the infinite nameless
colors he swallowed
to flaunt his white light

—*prism*

—◦◦◇◦◦—

Here I was, a star-nosed mole,
blind as the night was long
You pried them open
and the light spilled in
How can you now blame me
for wanting it all?

—*20/20 vision*

Can you be a Gemini
born in July?
Can you wake up wanting to
weave a crown of wildflowers,
as golden as the dawn
then slip silently from sunlight
to screen light?
Can you wear red lipstick,
dust your cheeks with rose
then fade into a gown as black
as a crow in a starless sky?
Can you light a cigarette and
love the way that it smells and
hate the way that it makes you taste?
Can you ache to paint the human body in the morning
and want to dissect it at night?
Can you crave silk, watercolor, moss, freesia, zin,
     clay, and clove
and
silver, espresso, moondust, blood, rubber,
     diamonds, and salt?
Can you need silence and screams
be silk and shard
sparrow and spider?
Can you be a Gemini
born in July?

—*dualing parts*

Keep your silver lining,
I'm looking for the gold

—*worth the weight*

Why do you sit alone
they ask
Because there is simply
not *enough* of me
to go around, dear

—*supply and demand*

In my presence
I demand decency
Please, leave your vices
at the door

—*high tea with a hypocrite*

Whom shall I thank for the dawn?
A master of your craft,
your tapestry,
exquisite
Although I'm afraid to inquire
the coin you will collect
in exchange for such
resplendent riches

—*excise tax*

—◇◇◇◇—

Truth, beauty, happiness, and peace
are all asymptotes
Yet I remain delusional
in swift pursuit of the horizon
Call it faith
Call it hope
Desperation
The truth is—
I never was very good at mathematics

—*to infinity*

Small

I love nothing more than when the world makes me feel small. Little reminders in a universal language I can only understand when I slow my heart and still my hands. Like the twinge in my neck when I arch to glimpse the crown of a redwood. The ache I feel on a cold black night under a mist of stars. The way the swollen belly of a mid-summer papaya dissolves bits of my tongue. How a single cell fissures into billions to form an entire being. The way my daughter sighs against my chest in a deep and dreamless sleep.

Just like a drop of water under a microscope, the wonderwork is invisible until we simply *focus*. Flowers have sex organs, because they, too, know desire. Even protons cradle children and lovingly call them quarks. Rain plinks on a tin roof during a summer squall and quiets every qualm. A virus subsisting on a single strand of RNA makes able-bodied men kneel and weep. A wood thrush sings an aria in a mossy dell, and my heart thrums staring at a kingdom of granite called Yosemite.

The signs are everywhere, earnest and bright. A brand-new human shares the evening sky with the light of ancient stars. A canyon, terraced with strata of sandstone and shale, boasts the intricate layers of its birthdays' cake. Dogs quietly show more compassion and loyalty than many human beings. The smell of fresh bread, kneaded under my mother's hands, puffs up on an open flame and makes all aches and pains disappear. Starlings perform synchronized acrobatics at dusk, and a family of geese makes a sign of peace in the sky as they carry on home.

Are you there? Make me feel small, I whisper, as the earth embraces me and answers in kind with a cold rain that dissolves my ego and quietly plumps the olives on the tree in front of my house.

GLUTTONY

They surfeited with honey and began
to loathe the taste of sweetness.

—William Shakespeare, *Henry IV*

A field of keloids grows on my back
self-cultivated
They want more
more
more
How else do I meet the demand?

—whip lash

———∞◇∞———

They claimed it a land of milk and honey
when they set the table for you and me
the umber of honey a thing of beauty
Theoretically
I thought it was milk that spoils
but that was naïveté
Faces soured, noses turned
when I sat down to feast

—black sheep

Glitz and glam
has never appealed to me
but *influence*
makes me salivate

When the delirium sets in
I don my coxcomb,
curtsy, and
take heart in the folly

One day
I will transfigure this world
fell, feckless, melancholy

—delusions of grandeur

———◦◦◇◦◦———

I have always been a wolf
in sheep's clothing,
but lately, I tire of the drag
I want to flaunt my teeth
and see the fear in their eyes
as I devour them
Whole

—bon appétit

I sleep well
with a belly full of poems

—sustenance

━━━━◦◦◇◦◦━━━━

Have you ever bitten
a peach
ripe as midsummer
Its juice dribbling
down your chin
in rivulets of nostalgia
Its flesh full of innocence
pink promise
sunshine
and memory of a time
before the suspicion
settled in?

—summer vacation

Summertime

It's summertime, and I'm steeped in nostalgia for all the lives that ran in parallel with my own that escaped me. I am so tired of cars. So utterly bored of boxy suburban Levittown eyesores checkered across cement-plated hills. So sick of screens, of routine, of debts, of duty.

Today, I want a plot twist. I want to make up a new name—something dreamy like Lucienne or Seraphina—and move to Italy. I want to pick fat, ripe tomatoes and feel their pulp squelch between my fingers as I crush them into a summer sauce. I want to till the land until the dirt beneath my fingertips becomes a permanent part of me. I want to savor food that I *witnessed* claw through the earth. I want to dip my hand into clay and mold a wobbly vase. I want to paint it with dahlias before I glaze and fire it into permanent imperfection. I want to learn how to hold a bow, to feel the hum of its tension as I pull back and shoot an arrow straight into the heart of any man of my choosing. I want to learn new, unfamiliar skills, like patience, bravery, and gentleness. I want to sing in a choir and feel the uncompromising chills of perfect harmony. I want to fish in a cool river under a hive of gnats and slap my neck in protest at their insistent companionship. I want to learn about wine and how its mouth, body, and legs seduce better than any person I've ever known. I want to smash every mirror so I no longer have to think about my face or what people expect of it. I want to walk alone at night without being afraid. I want to picnic on the crest of a mountain and fill my belly with fresh-baked gluten and alpine air. I want to taste fruits I can't pronounce and let their juices settle into my skin, sticky-sweet. I want to patent one of the dozen inventions floating in my head. I want to sit under the fading sun and read poetry, philosophy, and fantasy until I unravel into a beatific lightness. I want to learn the language of the birds, so I can thank them for easing the ache of each new morning. I want to jump in a getaway car, tear off my mask, and feel the raw wind rip through my hair and bite my cheeks—proof of life in a land of numbness.

They only hunger for a lyric,
because everyone loves a song

But I was born cursed,
mottled with feeling
and swollen with verse
with no tune to immortalize me

When does this compulsion
become insanity
as I whisper
incessantly
in riddles
into the dark?

—*dead poets society*

and so, I told them—
look, I know you're not doctors,
but living
is dying

if you won't eat the chocolate cake,
I can't help you

sometimes joy
is the medicine

—a spoonful of sugar

We all need something to devour
Some swallow whole their teams
others, the glow of their screens
and I
the narrow shafts of light
that filter in through the pines

All of us slaves
to the rituals that dampen
the sound of wails
carried in on the morning breeze

—*binge*

———◇◇◇———

Gluttony cackled in my face
when I said I was on a diet
Whiskey, highs
Sex, fries
Pick your poison
You're running out of time
No one is getting out of here alive

—*peer pressure*

Resuscitation

I love taking her out, this woman in front of me. I remind her that she is deserving, that no one can love her quite like I do. The rules for tonight are simple— no mirrors and no compromises. We see enough of both during the week.

We arrive in black, unapologetically taking up space. Our eyeliner is sharp enough to slit a throat. We spare no smiles, no simpers, and no expense. I ask her if she wants steak or shrimp. *Both*, she says, with a grin and a glint.

We demand that the martinis taste like the brine of the morning surf and that a thin veil of ice accompany olives bursting with bleu. We want the sting of the salt and the stench of the cheese to cleanse us. We want the vodka from the highest shelf. Tonight, we scoff at small talk and delight in denials as we brandish *no* like a bludgeon. We let it melt in our mouth and relish the way a word so small can feel so full on our tongue.

We are *famished*, and we have come to feast. We want the salad to smell of the mist beneath the redwoods, the mushrooms to taste like earth after rain. We want to hear the protest of fresh pepper-corns cracking in the mill. *Yes*, we want more bread. Make certain it's drowning in garlic butter.

We want the wine to tell us a tale of low-hanging plums and sweet black currants ripening under the Dog Star. No pinot-water tonight—we want wine as thick as blood clot and the emotion perpetually lodged in our throat. The filet must be velvet, the potatoes must be silk. And, though our viscera may protest, do not neglect the denouement! Bring us lavender, creme, and espresso—all the treats and tarts to indulge every sense. It has been a long week, so keep them coming. Make us moan. Tonight, we do not settle. We do not share.

We came here to dine till death. We leave here reborn.

Acknowledgments

Writing a book takes a village, and I owe mine my deepest gratitude.

To my husband, Brett, whose patience, flexibility, and quiet but unrelenting support made it possible to balance full-time medical careers and parenthood while completing this book. Inspiration doesn't respect schedules, so his willingness to shoulder the chaos of our home, businesses, and a toddler at a moment's notice to create space for my work is something I'll always be thankful for.

To my daughter, Maya, for her unconditional love and the joy that has saturated my life since her arrival.

To my parents, Anwar and Jabeen, who have always supported anything I've ever wished to pursue. If I told them I wanted to go to the moon, the only question they'd ask is, "Where can we get the parts to help you build the ship?" And in many ways, this book *has* felt like going to the moon—a journey into uncharted territory for someone who has dedicated the last twenty years of her life to medicine.

To my dad, especially, for introducing me to the world of poetry as a child—in Urdu, in English, in written verse, and in song.

To my friends, who unknowingly served as Mission Control: Kate, for your pep talks and guidance; Alyson and Gabriela, for knocking out my imposter syndrome before it got too bold in the ring; and Katherine, for your unwavering positivity and for being the hype girl every creative deserves.

To these, and to all the other people in my life, who have lifted, steadied, and believed in me, thank you for giving me the space to dream and the courage to write.

About the Author

Mariam Anwar Molani, DO, MBA, is a physician, scientist, and writer. A triple-board-certified pathologist, she completed her medical training at UT Southwestern in Dallas, Texas, and serves as a diagnostician and medical director for laboratories across the United States. Beyond medicine, she is a contemporary poet and essayist whose work explores themes of morality, power, and the intersections of science, nature, and art. She lives in Los Angeles with her husband, daughter, and geriatric wiener dog. This is her first book of poetry.